FIVE INPRINT POETS

Carolyn Tourney Florek, editor

foreword by Michael Lieberman

Mutabilis Press

Houston

The following works by Stan Crawford first appeared in other publications as noted:

"Harvest Sestina" in *Borderlands: Texas Poetry Review*
"Natural History" in *Illya's Gold*
"Blind Spot" in *Poet Lore*
"Gone to the Circus" in *Houston Poetry Review*

The following works by Varsha Shah first appeared in a slightly different form in the
following publication:

"Voices" and "In Other Words" in *Borderlands: Texas Poetry Review*

The name "Inprint" is used by permission of Inprint, Inc., a non-profit literary arts
organization that champions creative writing and reading in Houston through
workshops, reading series, community programs and other special events.

Book design and photography by Bob Florek and Carolyn Tourney Florek

Published by:
Mutabilis Press
3514 Deal St.
Houston, Texas 77025

Printed in the United States of America
by Gorham Printing, Rochester, Washington

Library of Congress Control Number: 2003110416
ISBN 0-9729432-1-8

FIVE INPRINT POETS

FOREWORD

"Notes Toward a Supreme Fiction," Wallace Stevens' great poem of exploration of the relation of poetry to the self and the world, ends with an epilogue in which Stevens talks more or less explicitly about what the poet's wisdom means to the man of action:

> The soldier is poor without the poet's lines,
>
> His petty syllabi, the sounds that stick,
> Inevitably modulating, in the blood.

Implicit in these lines is that Stevens himself, like the five poets in this anthology, lived both lives—the life of an active lawyer and insurance company vice president and the life of the poet. Poetry informed his life in the real world more directly than is generally imagined. The tension between the world and the world of the imagination (*mundo*) is everywhere in this poem. Like Stevens, James Adams, Stan Crawford, Thad Logan, Varsha Shah, and Elizabeth Wallace have lives beyond the creative writing academy as, respectively, a business consultant, lawyer, teacher, business analyst, and psychiatrist. They bring real world experience to poetry, the wisdom of the combatant, as Stevens would have it, and that of the parent, child and lover as well.

From the very first lines of the first poem by Adams to the last lines by Wallace, which Carolyn Florek has so thoughtfully selected and arranged, one senses Stevens' love of language, his inventiveness and precision, his struggle with how the two worlds are related.

Adams begins:

> Go on chandlers, burn your rhymes the
> long stemmed, round
> > or scented kinds . . .

And Wallace concludes:

> I can map
> his cake but not how
> he tastes it, eats it
> whether he discovers
> what is buried chest deep.

In between there is much thoughtfulness and passion—and inventiveness:

Crawford writes:

> By five A.M. your eyes
> went out like fireflies.
> I love you, off and on.

And Logan:

> What used to be you whispers at the door,
> My arms lengthen down the stairs.
> I embrace what I can of you,
> Disappearing.

And Shah:

> Making love meant babies.
> A woman meant not much
> on her own,
> or when left alone.

Stevens would have been proud of his legacy. I have been privileged as the leader of an Inprint poetry workshop for the past several years to learn from these poets. They have enriched me as a person and a poet. They bring an immersed reflectiveness about the real world that is held, if not uniquely then most touchingly, in the mind of the practitioner/poet. Now, reader, you can share my good fortune.

Michael Lieberman

CONTENTS

Introduction

We met in a workshop at Inprint led by poet Michael Lieberman. I first met Jim Adams, Varsha Shah, and Elizabeth Wallace in the fall of 2001. I decided to take the workshop again in 2002 and there met Stan Crawford and Thad Logan. Between workshops we have regularly met in groups of our own, reading and critiquing our developing poems.

During this time each of us has accumulated a body of work, stacking them up, not only in our imaginations, but on paper, on computers, and in each other's ears and thoughts.

To actually write poetry is a strange combination of courage and ego. Each of us craves the reader's attention and understanding. We wrestle with our inner demons and angels, struggling to make a beautiful and necessary art. Many of us do this for years, completely alone, not ever daring to share the deepest thoughts expressed in our poems. We are afraid. We are terrified that our poetry, which gives us identity, will be judged ordinary.

Then perhaps there comes a day when we dare to take a workshop. It is a time commitment, for most of us have full-time jobs already. It is an emotional commitment as well. The moment we first read our poetry aloud to a group is a moment of extreme anxiety. Worse yet, is the silence that often follows. And more silence and more, until, if we are fortunate, a kind, but firm voice breaks this intimidating silence with questions like:

"What is this poem about? Who is the speaker in this poem? Who are they speaking to?" Or, unbelievable, but music to the ears of the poet— "Why does this poem work?"

Do these questions make us better poets? Or do they make us better readers of poetry? We poets come to a workshop with our handful of poems, apprehensive but determined. In the process, we learn that we can become better poets by reading the poetry of others. And this is what we want to become, better poets.

On the last day of my first workshop, a group of poets read their work, each with a unique voice, each with the courage to speak aloud. Before he let us go, Michael Lieberman said, "This is as good as it gets."

Here are the poems by five Inprint poets, five out of many, but like no other. Five poets that I have had the supreme pleasure to read, to hear and to begin to know. I am forever grateful and changed by their gifts to all of us.

Carolyn Tourney Florek

JAMES ADAMS

James Adams is a poet maintaining residence in Houston, Texas. He has studied creative writing at the University of Texas at Austin, UCLA, and the Université Paris IV (la Sorbonne). Adams has been awarded poetry prizes, foreign and domestic. His poems have been translated into French, Spanish, Dutch, Ukrainian, and Russian.

Adams describes himself as "a quite private person who prefers discussing actual poems rather than actual poets." He comments upon his poetry as "hopefully—inclusive of a certain meaningful wordplay, a van Gogh ear for the surprise in rhyme and cadence, a conveyance of multiplicity of depth in subject matter through the tool of ambiguity." Amongst his favorite poet-writers he counts Dylan Thomas, Emily Dickinson, Robert Graves, Edna St. Vincent Millay, Sylvia Plath, Apollinaire, Shakespeare, Donne, Simonides, and David. "My chief dislikes are people who are cruel to animals, snobs, and poetry critics who imagine they know more about a poet's work than the poet."

Adams is a member of the Academy of American Poets, the Writer's Guild, and Scribes. He is a direct lineal descendant of the Wadsworth poetical family. He has served as senior editor for various technical publications. His interests encompass grand felines, parasitology, and tennis.

CHANDLERS

Go on chandlers, burn your rhymes the
long stemmed, round
            or scented kinds
it doesn't matter
            no one cares
for golden lengths of wickened air.

Go on candlers, turn your signs
to fickle, nymph-held
            silver limes
it doesn't matter
no one listens
to silent cheeks who-speak in glisten.

Go on now, without:

it wouldn't do to give them handles
for which could grasp blue-roaring candles?

You Know My Heart (To You Belongs)

You know my heart to you belongs
      I brake it thus, unsteady
—through all this year's unbidden songs
my scrawl's to you, aready;

Such blood unveined pumps
      to this stage
I break its walls-confetti,
and though these years forbidden page
my scrawls to you, asteady;

You know my heart to you belongs
      I take it cares ajettied
And love this love
so filled in strongs—
Of pen, of pen-calmed eddies —

CHILDREN'S DECEMBER NIGHTSONG

I can't remember
      little fleeces
but in the moon
      last midnight geeses

a-skying high in
      fowling pieces
fresh flown from turkeys
      (or is it Greeces?)

These eves hold
hands in timeless ceases
sleep laden eyelash
pearl pelisses.

I can't November
      little fleeces
for in the moon
      last midnight geeses

they seemed to wing
      blue feathered nieces
and looking up
      fall fell to peaces.

MUSINGS INTERRUPTED

Good even knight
        Fama pledged to me
forgive these trampl'g
        divinities

We could not help
adore thee here
with sword ashined
and thought unsheared.

Erato, Calliope
        I started, speak'd:
ye skin-glows fine
        lip fiery cheek'd—

No interrup-tion
Euturpe's done,
for I adure ye
one in one;

then whom seeks whom
demurred these beauties
arrest this flight,
refrain such duties.

So with a touch
Polyhymnia sway'd
our hands-loved on—
azured aways.

GRASP VENUS

I would have loved you like Colossus
      —but you wouldn't have it—
I would have grasped Venus
      and made her dance
a two step tango.

All this you knew and I know:

love you wanted Euripides to write
you hunted fiststunned heroes to sing
psalms at Valhalla, immortal couplets
to reach out fingerspread
      thumbscrew touch overhead

a bridge of mercury tears
wingskipping Olympus
and Hera's reach, immoral
couplets forging
a golden practicum,

backhand Aphrodite
squeeze bronze ambrosia
press Cytheric foam
clutching dovetail myrtles
into a curl
garland-discus to arc to

your feted feet reputed
      repeated
I would have loved you like
I would have loved you like
I would have loved you like
      TriColossus

but you wouldn't have it.

BEEFISH

We swam the freshman
swim—long ago, longing
laugh-open, foaming, turning
over   to float
in an ocean of honeys.

Beefish, all tails and fin
flings, brushcuts sharp
to translucent beeswings

against-crush hearts
and our beautiful,
beautiful bee's
stings.

My soul
      still-buzzes
            near you

as pollenbit
butternutsmear you;
thrill-sticky, cracked
ambered over
and racked into
these

drowned
rutbraided
antennæ.

SELF PORTRAIT

He said the soul of Willem
        van Gogh flew
off the wall at the *Musée d'Orsay*
in starving crackles
gilt-ridden window frames
hung whipwires—

red dashes of brush,
to green turn blue, to black
flecked like a tender hand
flicking tiny bits of eyelash
        purpled beard-hairs on
thin-generous cheeks
in genius'd streaks—

on to his delicate knuckles
down his pointing index
of netherland-ivory fingers
flowing dark dutchmaster paint
onto bright cottonpound canvas;

staggered by the shudders
of knowledge
        he would remain
unknown, posthumous
doomed with
this incredible
ache-wondrous
sad and inedible
beauty.

18

YES TO NO (AN ANTHOLOGY)

'I assume we have your permission
          to publish.'
Yes?

'The line is bad—can you hear?'
No, how many?

'Five of them.'
A wave of disbelief.

'They're quite good—others
          here agree.'
A flush of pride.

'The only thing is—'
Delay, of course.

'—we want to change the title,'
A flush of nothing.

'from _______ to _______.'
That will alter the meaning.

'This is a condition precedent for inclusion.'
A pause with no-answer.

'The connection—did you hear?'
Yes.

'And you understand?'
Yes; yes.

'Yes to the change, or
          yes to the understanding?'

Yes to no.

A Poet's Reply
to Ivy Leagued Critics Drinking in Los Angeless

Attend C'lubmia, *Havard*
Princess-by-tonnes
—'tis certain you're a genius;
and's long as fools
        view emperor's clothes,
you've empressive gown-length
        splenius.

For as you lever crania high
arch hairy nose near'r heav'n;
you might remember Christ's reply
        to the geniuses of leaven.

Pronounce my lines ungrammar'd, dull
        and freely re-arrange then
attack my cats' Afrika-lulled,
        claim cherokee deranged them.

My friends, who know you
        tell me true
you're jealous 'till you're bare,
your Schools I won't fit art-insides;
from this genius
        you're spare.

But the rhymes, o bitterns, leave
my rhymes alone; such chitons
you'll are unmindful, for Emily
Dylan, William B,
these tritons judge:
not whinefulls.

Notes:
"splenius": longitudinal muscles in the rear of the human neck, allowing upward tilt.
"bittern": 1. heron-like marsh bird with a booming cry, usually feeding at or near the shoreline;
        2. (*slang*) a bitter compound used in adulterating alcoholic beverages.
"chiton": ancient Greek tunic, full-length, usually worn by women or elderly men, sometimes by
        youths or workmen.
"triton": Greek sea god.

20

PIG

When I reached the lowest
point a poet
          may I
entered a con test
honestly believing I's
wouldwind.

And off I oinked
five poems
(with appropriate fees)
to the tha—that's
all folks
at the pigpen.

On the big night out
a-doored I met
          ghostess writers
reminding me
my kermit's life was best
bug-eyed zoners
waving their latest
pulp paperbacks
like duchess-proofs
shining look-I'm-verified hooks,
cook and shook
bespeckled husbands,
the unstrong
faux-ettes tonight
like me.

Ah *ja* I slopped up the wine
chic-crunched the wafers
chewed the spud

I made the chit-fat
muzzle dipped and
fingerbowled troughs.

I made myself fetch
I made my self-retch
spoons for organizing officers
hum hellohowRU-hiptoones
          to Lorna Loons,

I-spotted expectants
hurling disinfectants
the polite dinner call of small,
          small talk.

I was grubbing
for *phats* 'n thisnthat's
Friedas Freds and Pats
on the backs touching
hip truffles; hoove-stepping
to cool muffles rooting
the groove-prove
plush piles

As I said
I couldn't wallow lower
I couldn't be more untrue

I couldn't break apart ever
more promises
more delicacies
more tears
more thinbellied gutburns
more vows—

my hand hurt
my heart burst
fine, integrity-laden parts
warning me to get out get smart
escape, go,
save myself, the bacon
anything

warning me
my ears
too late
had begun to grow
pointed, my nose
pumping in parcels
unannointed and flattening
down disjointed
with every award announced
with each forced smile

in loud peals
to liquored squeals
I clapped my halves
spread salve-oinkments
trumpeted herd-slaps
sowed
        cut-eyed askances

grunting.

STAN CRAWFORD

Stan Crawford is an attorney who practices civil trial law in Houston, Texas. He lives in the Heights with his wife, Dawn, and Java, their dysfunctional Chow-Labrador mix. His two daughters live in a small town in southern Louisiana, and visit Houston frequently. He has a B.A. from Brown University, where he studied poetry with Michael Harper, and a J.D. from the University of Texas.

Crawford began writing poetry again in 1998, after an interruption of twenty-five years. He has recent work published or forthcoming in *The Comstock Review, Borderlands: Texas Poetry Review, Poet Lore* and *Houston Poetry Review.* He has attended workshops at Inprint in Houston and Gemini Ink in San Antonio, with Mike Lieberman, Alan Ainsworth, Sarah Cortez and Tony Hoagland. In 2003, Crawford was a finalist for the Jane Kenyon Poetry Prize awarded by Hamline University in St. Paul, Minnesota, and won first prize in the Dallas Poets Community's Sixth Annual Open Poetry Competition, 2001.

"The poets whose work I return to again and again, and whose influence I feel most strongly, include Lowell, Bishop, Kinnell and Stafford. I try to combine autobiographical detail and metaphor with their guidance in mind, to achieve a strength of expression through personal experience translated into images that distance and clarify."

NATURAL HISTORY

On my weekends we'd go back
to where things stayed in place:
the criss-cross bricks wedged tightly
over sprawling roots, white marble steps
worn down like soap, the neoclassic doorway
and inside, a funnel for donations
curved to keep coins up on edge,
faster and faster, spinning through
an aperture into a void.

My girls were younger, more predictable.
They always went first
into the hall of Texas wildlife scenes
lined up like ice cubes in a tray—
a cougar posed, muscles tensed
to leap on a fearful mule deer
and rake apart its neck;
coyotes arranged in a canyon mouth,
about to tear into eastern cottontails.

In time we stopped going back.
I moved away, then they did.
My mind still adds a last tableau:
a nursery scene lit by a lamp,
a sleeping child, a crib, and the woman
who was my wife leans over
to savor the baby's durable breath,
my hand frozen upon her shoulder
our eyes unmoving and unmoved
almost the final time
before we unbraced into our own purposes,
no longer useful to each other.

BLIND SPOT

There was a time you drove
through summer's furnace, hermetically sealed,
listening to your own tune,
some golden oldie, and when you checked
the rear view mirror showed
no impediment

so you crossed the line
and someone's heart skipped, fusing
his hand to his horn a fraction
before the crash, but you never saw him,
never signaled
a change

and the time your son or daughter
said with a face clenched like a fist,
I will never forgive you for that, never,
but you didn't understand the reference,
your mind an empty plate
for this course

as well as the evening your love
gazed distractedly out the window and toward the sky
again and again, but when you looked out
there was nothing, just her reflection
in the windowpane, pale
and darkness behind.

See how the mirror holds the world:
street lights glide in reverse,

cables swoop backward, heavy with words,
cars race toward places you've left
as trees spar silently in the wind.

You see everything you've come through
except your own part.
You can drown in water so clear
it reflects no light.

How I See It

This morning's light
holds its shoes and tip-toes
past the windows.

Soon recycling
trucks will come for everything
we go through twice.

Three lemons on
the kitchen counter keep
a quiet vigil.

Someone spilled
gin and a little tonic on
the only map.

We lit midnight
cigarettes. Acrid
lacy smoke.

That raccoon who fled
up our pecan tree never
came back down.

By five A.M. your eyes
went out like fireflies.
I love you, off and on.

Observed in Belize

You saw him first
beside the sandy track
puddled with rain
white as café au lait--
a blue crab still as an exposed root,
one claw held high,
the pincer torn,
his gray meat open to the wind.

Then I looked at starlight
metastasized how many centuries ago,
given a familiar name:
Invader of Shallows,
Breathing Bone, Crab Nebula.
Muzzy pricks of light
over restless palm trees
shadowing your crab.

Let us close our eyes and dream
one eye acute enough
to see particular each instant lit
by stars exploded years ago,
kind enough to capture with a glance
the broken crab in shadow
by the tin-roofed shack
dispensing Chinese takeaway.

Harvest Sestina

October already—a very long distance
from spring. Knives sharp for the harvest.
Autumnal processions and daughters to see
and I went, holding the wheel with one hand
along roads that twisted, broke and rose,
unfurling ahead like concrete sails

running before the wind. Nothing to assail
for awhile. Stars salted the cobalt distance.
My daughters, a/k/a Snow White and Rose
Red, chose their gowns for the harvest.
Melons, pumpkins and late corn at hand.
This year's ad hoc royals to see.

My orbit taught new ways to see,
to tack into the wind, to sail
crosswise. The temperature stung my hands
too near the nest. A needful distance
away, roadside stands held the harvest.
A woman with a tumor red as a rose

near her eye stacked fruit in serried rows,
composing her still life. Her son could see
her designs as he counted cash from the harvest.
A king with his chest puffed out like a sail
started off the parade. Signs in the distance
said *Vote for Jesus—His Kingdom at Hand.*

Then a band, and the waving hands
of young women in formal green, white, rose.
A catfish moon low in the distance,
as boys with bad haircuts strained to see
their sisters pass. The tomato sun sailed
west, simmering over the harvest.

The road was fringed with cuts from the harvest,
uncollected by any restraining hand.
The tired king followed his sagging sail
of a belly to bed. The pale moon rose
over the swaying cane. I could see
waves like Evangeline's hair in the distance.

A rose in hand fuzzes with dust. My girls,
see them glide, whispering rumors of sails.
Not so long a distance to harvest time.

GONE TO THE CIRCUS

for Dawn

Lillian Leitzel enters the ring,
and a mad-eyed parrot in a cage
on a porch a block away from me
hangs upside down and screeches, mocking
industrious martins and hip-hop jays.

I turn a page, and Lillian grips
the rings (her palms dry as ash);
she begins to turn like a human propeller
and no one below can stop staring
until the cymbals crash.

She taught her body to spin like this
by slipping her shoulder out of the socket,
which now she can do like doffing a hat
for she is the Queen of the Roman Rings;
caution is dust in her pocket.

Then you wordlessly tease away
my book with a look that could singe
the afternoon clouds into caramel. We dis-
locate each other; the air crystallizes
and fills with calliope fringe

and an emerald skink continues to lounge
outside upon our porch rail,
consuming the self it has sloughed away
chewing its old skin with freakshow calm
savoring the tail

as Lillian spins. A woodpecker hen
pursues her mate up through a riddled tree
and into the sky (your light
light blue eyes).
Day of resisted gravity.

Cain's Complaint

Our deepest enemies are closest—
not threatening in the way
we may read about abstractedly
in our morning paper,
but right beside us, smirking
as we walk by to get coffee, or
humming wearisome tunes,
always getting to the bathroom before we do.
Mrs. Smith surrenders her pistol to the cops.
She's aerated her husband's spleen
because he wouldn't quit
putting the orange juice in the refrigerator
in front of the milk.
Grit in an oyster won't always seed pearls.

What really chapped Cain,
more than Abel's certainty he was the beloved,
more than his dung-dropping goats,
were the jokes,
like when they were hunting,
and Cain said, "We're not getting any ducks,
I wonder why,"
and Abel was all like,
"I don't know.
Let's throw the dog higher."

And then,
when Cain's wind-chosen figs
and pomegranates tumid with juice
were rejected by God,
Who preferred a lamb
with neck slashed and bleeding,
white fleece vandalized,

Abel's goofy, bloody grin....
Darkness drowned every bowl,
every wineskin inside Cain's tent.
He suddenly thought
his rage was a source of light,
and split Abel's skull under the furious sun

and God, in turn, banished Cain forever
to a suburb of ravens, dust devils and thorns.
Cain left (disobedience was not his sin),
yet marked forever as one of God's own—
self-absorbed, radioactive with anger—
an integral part of the nuclear family.

PROCESSIONAL

Our feet will teach the road the way to go.
Beneath our names for things are other names
until we reach the place we do not know.

On a day like others we've been shown,
one thing is changed, and nothing is the same.
Our feet will teach the road the way to go.

A seam of slate may verge with soapstone.
Memories will merge into our dreams
until we reach the place we do not know.

Above, the sky is vacant, and below
the blind and halt are gardening. Though lame,
our feet will teach the road the way to go.

Under winter trees, new seed is sown.
Our breathing blends together at the bloom
that grows inside the place we do not know.

The forms our empty hands recall, drawn
from harrowed air. A world is framed.
Our feet will teach the road the way to go
until we reach the place we do not know.

THAD LOGAN

Thad Logan teaches in the English Department at Rice University. Her husband Eric Lueders teaches English at Houston Community College and is currently on the board of the *Gulf Coast* literary magazine. Their daughter Helen attends The University of Southern California.

Logan has a B.A. from the University of California in Santa Barbara, and a Ph.D. from Rice. She studies and teaches Victorian literature and culture. Her book, *The Victorian Parlour: A Cultural Study*, was published by Cambridge University Press in 2001. She is the author of several articles and papers exploring the relationship of Victorian people, places, and things. Her interest in poetry began when she first read William Butler Yeats' poem "The Lake Isle of Innisfree" at fifteen. Poetry by William Blake, Christina Rossetti, and Ezra Pound has also been important to her, as have the songs of Bob Dylan, her experiences as an actor and director, and her various travels. She has recently begun to write poetry for publication, and this is her first collection of poems.

KATIE'S

The Steinmanns were beautiful
(Except the homely father,
And the ancient, hump-backed granny)
Skin like magnolias, even the boys, hair like night.
And they lived like I had never seen.
Their house was pointy, wood and stone,
The living room pink and purple
With a big piano, and a metronome,
Books in the library, mess on the stairs,
Sewing in the dining room
The house musky, and alive,
Irish, and Catholic.

Katie was "Little Miss Cotton,"
I have her picture still, a frilly dress, a parasol,
black eyes.
By seventh grade, she had a hundred lipsticks.

One afternoon in October,
I knocked on the back door, turned the knob
And found her mother
In the panelled breakfast room,
Like a dark Vermeer
With a birthday cake for Katie's brother
Putting on little black candles,
        Little wax cats,
The light around her swooning.

SAINT LUCY OF SYRACUSE VOWED TO BE CHASTE

and was so tormented by a young man
who worshipped her eyes
that she pulled them out
and sent them to him
on a platter.

Perhaps you thought I didn't see you there
Hiding behind the church door
Pen in hand.

Perhaps you imagined your poetry
Would open me like a rose.

Ah, my lips, my hair, my white skin, my blue eyes . . .

Now look your fill
I'll see only God.

The Pavillon DuBarry

1774

Lying nearly senseless now, the King, the Bien-Aimé,
remembers the trees at Louveciennes.
Not the stunted bourgeois trees along the Rue de la Machine,
Pruned to a standstill,
But the frivolous, beautiful trees of the park,
Framing the pavilion, arching their exquisite branches
Over the soft grey stone.

He remembers the lush geometry of the lawn in Spring.
Between the fine green and the white daisies,
It seemed there was no hard thing
left in the wide world.
On the frieze the amoretti woke and stretched,
the sun in the east warming them to life.
One by one they floated down,
Fragrant and pink as petals dropping lightly through the air,
Coming to rest on the grass.

1793

Long since, those little loves slowly made their sad return.
Grey mists haunt the gardens now, and the rain seeps in.
Madame has outlived her protector:
At Paris the blade drops,
And here in Louveciennes, leaves scatter
across the empty floor.

1967

Spring again, irrepressible, heart-rending
The pavilion now a school.
I'm sixteen and learning fast.
The days go by like roses,
Blissfully opening
Fragrantly falling away.

But this day the bloom holds
For the moment, and for the moment
The light shines through the green world,
Purely blessed, and blessing.

We are laughing on the lawn,
Your black hair in the daisies.
Here in Louveciennes
There is no god but love.

SOLFATARA

Heat, bird shadows,
Sun blasting the caldera.
Just a little way from the café,
The old crater spreads itself.
Here the ground is hollow,
It's surface gritty, saltish,
grey and laced with sulphur.

Here the little mouths whisper.
I bend and cup my hand,
Where Judith shows me,
and feel the warm, wet breath.
Her silver rings are tarnishing.

Higher up, the hissing vent.
"Sybilla, Sybilla"
we might cry, but
Answers blow uphill, away.

HAUNTING

Wet pavement, bits of leaf, twig, drowned worm,
        worldstuff.
Empty house, dark street, edgy moon.
Wind at an open window.

My eyes, my mouth
Burn in the darkness of my face,
ruining.

The body unmaking, the tape running backward,
bones unknitting.
In the long dark I linger, soft along the windowpanes,

What used to be you whispers at the door,
My arms lengthen down the stairs.
I embrace what I can of you,
Disappearing.

Evening, and the breezes come,
Lifting the silk ribbons.
The bridge is dressed for a summer night;
Lanterns strung along its wooden arches,
Shining peach and apricot into the quiet stream.

Tables are set beside the water
Under the willow trees.
Wine flows under the open moon
And the swifts circle overhead
Feasting on the sky.

Children run along the bridge. We hear the pattle
Of their shoes, and the crickets
Jingling. Out in the darkness, green and yearning,
The tendrils of the honeysuckle
Reach out for the rose.

NIGHTMARE

Jagged lines fork along the pavement
Like dark branches overhead.
I dream the street cracks open, and
There is a man down below,
Making a potion.

Then we are in the dining room,
We have dinner
And I try not to remember.
But I do, and there he is
In the yard, outside the window,
In his round house.
He sees me.

Around the table they keep talking, the big ones.
I don't want to be where they are not,
In the emptiness between their bodies,
Alone with this stranger
Running down the road.

The Right Bank

Once when I came back to Paris
I stopped at the wrong end of the Ile de la Cité.
I had a good view of the river,
I could imagine the curve it took
And how the city spread itself to the South and West.
That's where we'd lived.
Then something shifted under me,
As if the little island were a boat,
And all I wanted was to go there
To get up and go home.
My mother would be there, my sister,
My father would come in,
It wasn't far, it would be just the same.
It seemed it would be just the same,
And all I had to do was fly across the leafy streets,
To fly across the river,
But instead I stood there crying, on the other side.

Under the Patterned Cotton

In the big room she moves along the mirrors;
The air is hot with candles and the breath of dancers,
And I watch while the music lifts and twirls her,
The hem of her skirt curling around her heels
Like a ragged, hungry wind.

Lightly he rests his hand on her back.
The mirrors multiply that touch
It flashes out and finds me
In my little velvet chair,
Here at the limits of the evening.

I feel the delicate, inviting friction
As the fabric barely moves against the surface of her skin,
And the faint damp warmth at the S-curve of her spine,
The strength of muscle and bone under the surface,
The quick beats of her heart.

The live connection troubles my peace
sets my nerves ringing
Like the strings of the violins,
Makes little pizzicato stabs
Like the points of her silver shoes.

AFTER CAVAFY

"Half-past twelve . . .
How the time has passed.
Half-past twelve . . .
How the years have passed."
So the old poet wrote
In Alexandria.

Now for me the late-night candle
The wine, the time gone
And the long years wavering, indistinct.

Once a boy I knew
knew he was dying,
And he said, at the end,
" I didn't think it would come so soon."
And me, I did not think this kind of night
Would come so soon.

How fine they were, dark-eyed, or blue
How warm their skin
Hands pale or olive . . .
What touch could do . . .
How kisses fired the mind.

But these memories
Begin to loose their wrappings,
and drift off, one by one, along the sand,
a little parade
fragrant, musical
departing.

SUMMER VACATION

It's June, and Memo and I
ride across America.

Cornfields stretching from morning to night.
Passing the towns we can hear the bells at the crossing,
See the chrome on the cars shining in the sun,
The children waving.

I'm lucky to be on the train, in the narrow room,
On the stiff, scratchy upholstery.
In the tiny bathroom there are funny square faucets,
And the scary place at the bottom of the toilet,
The place where, when you flush it, it opens
And you see the stones on the ground going by so fast, so fast,
Before it shuts again.

In the late afternoon we come to a city
Where the light is sad.
Our train creaks, slows, stops. We wait.
There is a funny feeling, something is happening
Another train! So close to the window!
Gone again. We wait.
There's a jolt, a jerk back, then forward.
Slow, then faster, we go on.

One day we know it's the last day.
In the afternoon, we come to Cin-cin-atti
And then, late, to Parkersburg.
At midnight we stand in the aisle by the open window.
We can see the leaves come almost inside.
No place else is cool and dark
Like West Virginia.

VARSHA SHAH

Born and brought up in the western state of Gujarat, India, Varsha Shah immigrated to the U.S. in 1974 and currently lives in Houston, Texas with her family. She is a finance accounting professional who finds her fulfillment in poetry.

Her formal exposure to the craft of Western poetry began in 1998 at an Inprint workshop. She has studied with poets Alan Ainsworth, Derick Burleson, Michael Lieberman, and Lorenzo Thomas.

In 1999 Varsha was a featured poet in the *Houston Poetry Fest*. Her work is forthcoming in *Borderlands: Texas Poetry Review, The Texas Observer, Houston Review* and *Houston Poetry Review*. She has given readings for Voices Breaking Boundaries, Houston International Poetry, and Women in Visual and Literary Arts. Varsha writes poetry in English and Gujarati. Recently, her poetry and an essay won first place in a competition held by the Gujarati Society of Dallas-Fort Worth.

VOICES

Forget all harassing noises,
A voice says.
So I quit the crowd to model
in *sari* draped over a mini skirt.
You see, they call the *bindi* a dot on the forehead.
It is not a tattoo on the heel
nor a ring on the navel or finger.
It is my third eye.
I wake up to walk through the ceiling,
Nibble, sun and suspend my bilingual tongue.
A fly inside wall, No more.
I toss and mousse my hair, shun all that is vanilla.
Let the moon ruffle me once in a blue evening.
In the driveway, I join the stars' gossip—
We telltale and mingle for there is no escape from
What we say and what they hear,
What they speak and what we know.
I bend over fallen notes
sketching hope with broken pencils,
hear the sand rustle, let the birds bicker.
Even a fading word hisses to be heard.
I flip directories, poring over dictionaries
praise the unlisted to behold the undefined.
I paint with shadows, says the voice,
Contour me nude with a meteoric flash,
my eclipsed face in a jubilant profile.
Step aside O reason, my goddess exclaims,
feel my soil-like rawness, she says,
drench her in the monsoon's commune.
Go open my spice box for that vociferous cry.

LITTLE BLACK DRESS

She finds a woven evening inside raw silk
pondering over crêpe de chine, taffeta and chiffon—
the small scooped neck seamed to a half-moon back.
Perfect curves darned to a maiden waist
carved from black marble descending
firm, flowing knees.

Bosom tucked inside dainty waist,
the trimmed shoulders hold up like a bolero
postured for the dance, the back drop
just deep enough to swallow
body's light into a becoming night.

Tiny roses fashioned in satin,
their embroidered eyes hold heat
the three-way mirror carries—
queries that transcend skin folds, shapes
the motherhood defies, twisting answers
to archetype standards: how long must they fit
her body and its contrived images?

On a Circular Route

Little has changed at the familiar bus-stand.
An omelet vendor still waits on transiting fares.
Neat rows of eggs in his stall ready to go like dominos,
to fry with onions and chilies on a smoldering skillet.
A bull pees against the depot-wall a few feet away,
dust kicked with his hooves clouds passengers
shuffling without complaint.
A bull has its right in public.

The route circles the old Ahmedabad
and her moods; people, dark and the light.
Riders old and new to the city's oddities
rarely revolt at traffic jolts or halts,
resigning at the destined stops,
leaving pollution, zoning, the weather up to destiny.
Resiliency rules here; it is the way of living.

Inhale this spectrum: the potpourri of passengers—
brightly clothed villagers, urban commuters debating
about communal riots, political parties and the cost of living.
Each grabs a seat, indifferent about class or the caste.
Exhale: each time you find or discard
the experience you did not choose.

A cop still dresses from bottom to top in British Raj khaki.
A college gal in cut-offs flirts with a pal in Polo,
a turbaned elder keeps deferential gap, wary
not to touch my thigh as the bus turns,
watching my non-resident manners furtively.

The bus conductor makes my favorite click-punch music
each time he cuts a ticket from his box-like book with metal covers—
not a single note changed, pressing it down in my palm,
jingling the change and ticketing just the way he did years ago
when I used to board at this suburban station
returning via bus number 60
day after day after day
on a commute that felt like chanting
Om…om…om…in a circular rhythm.

SCAFFOLDS

(for D.T.)

As the morning blustered outside,
He lay frozen dark inside
A warm brightly-lit room, deaf to the eulogy
Offered with incense, flowers and fruit.

Chants rose from a language, pictorial
Words invoked familiar spirits.
Sounds made from the body's five winds
Deadened inside, left the mourners mute.

Calligraphic songs wept in diagonal flow
Looking for shelter on red rice paper,
Bamboo sticks casting intricate pyres,
Bones ready to restore body with the earth.

What's occult drifted from the father,
Towers of ink, trees & tepees,
Geometry unfolding a landscape of loss,
The daughter wailed in praise, son hailed "O Father!"

The pictures transcribed possibilities
In a script grander than trophies, or
Memorials sculpted from marble, or cast in bronze
He must have considered once lying awake.

LIQUID BOND

(Celebrating Kiki Smith's art titled:
"Twelve Silvered Glass Water Bottles Arranged in A Row: Representing
Urine, Mucus, Tears, Diarrhea, Milk, Saliva, Semen, Vomit, Pus,
Sweat, Oil, Blood")

I remember my floor tremble with pain
how the sky crashing with thunder
trades blues with earth.
I thought of us as two hummingbirds
drowning in nectar, one universe
transcending the elemental species.

My tears spoke to you inside the chamber
as we sweated and salivated together.
You even dared urinate in my womb
caving like a pustule breaking my bloody pear—
in its liquid bond you grew.

The mucus you breathed out
left you pure, unperturbed like oil
floating on water you broke loose.

Come, celebrate my milk.
Let us drink
        to the opaque silver of his semen.

Closets Redeemed

Things we lug for years unaware
how time stores us in belongings
we let go from the days' confluence.

The clothes children outgrew,
shoes that transported now weary
relieved from confinement on crowded back racks.
Songs that lulled and buoyed around the crib—
Old McDonald's Farm and Mother Goose's
madness once ruled motherhood's veins,
inscribing new maps on the palms—
Each universe now a satellite without orbit.
That quintessential bundle of diapers
unworn, looks archaic
ought to part off the shelf.
The yellow radio still yells jingles, crisp
like morning glories on a lawn
faded pink and distant like the dawn
when I meted out a piece of my youth.
Little doctor's kit, still fit
for a toddler's fat fingers can't go yet.
He used to take my pulse
gingerly jabbing a shot in my shoulder
planting his pouty face into my breast.

On the driveway, spring bugs in tandem
chase around the stories to read,
jumbled puzzles need sorting—
Some will have to wait for the next round—
Ah, it's fun playing God.

IRONING CURLS

That evening the three of us combed our hair
grooving between generations
chic and the classic.

Thirteen,
In swerving braids, black jasmine helixes
holding the girlhood's wild card,
The soiree kicked off with a sandalwood dab
under lobes, rosewater splash over arms.
Saris our confetti wrapped below navel—
          Our indulgence rattled uncles' world
that accepted only the prudent.

You two ironed your curls,
          the electric wand teasing tangles
from silk to a straightened hay sheath.
We giggled, watching it return to a cranky mass.

We rehearsed in velvet black
          Our matchmaking aunts forbade
gossiping on a porch about destined mates,
faulty stars and the holy colors - red and white.
          Black meant mourning, not wedding,
they would say, pick an auspicious moment,
and enfold your fate.
One told us a story of an astrologer
          whose wife died on their wedding night,
cursing karma and its irony, the unknown.

As if to defy the unknown, you two shunned
dresses custom-defined, tossing what made no statement.
We laughed and tumbled in sashes and slips,
          bare shoulders all evening,
our arms autumn's new gold, glowing
     thighs not shy about the slits.

WHITE COAT RITE

(for Pooja)

Orange clouds somersault
into a blue-white twilight sheet.
Tidal laughter cracks open the shore,
          its white noise dancing about
the indolent palms fanning their airy hands.
Moon at her zenith —
light and water hold each other tightly,
the horizon a dark strip of day's film.
Frothy water fringed over rippling hills
the seagulls climb in unison.

In their noisy parley
I remember the mid-day shuffle
of white coats, the initiation inside auditorium.
Scores of angels ready to take off
holding Hippocrates in their coat pockets,
in the gentle tap of their marching steps,
in the dazzling sleeves each a pair of promising wings.
"First Do No Harm,"
my little girl, a freshman, avows
striding resolutely into the tide of healers.

The waves frolic,
white shudder
laughing, transiting,
flapping coats riding on light's sail

POET'S MARKET

Buy me, sell me, rent me, use me
In the name of your twenty-six letters,
musing each vowel with thumping fingers
on the brink of a crater, roadside café,
rendered by thousands,
in noble conjugations or base combinations.

Remember: I am
the assembly of word-lords,
judge de millennia
borders abound.
What came to you has surpassed
You beyond muse,
the men and women of letters
I take you for your words.

Dream, dream.
Be wise, be foolish, re-feel and revise, coast and discourse
at the pond's edge and sky's end inside your page.

Beware: You're only a ware in my realm—
My bazaar's open to the novice as well
Nobody, the known— Definition is yours.

Send me lines, organic and non.
Take a chance in the name
of obscure stars, for the sake of stars,
by the seekers of stars.
I am a mammoth commercial
in freedom's province.

ARS POETICA

You trouble me too much.

I agonize your landing—
I dread your departure, always abrupt.

In your disguise I ache
from not quickening that instant.

You stay back, I'm destitute.
Fallen on a leaf a multi-headed beast,

I can't unfold enough
to enfold you in whole.

Promise me—
No one will dare you from me.

To be free, I must flee
from hangout to our hideout,

From bourgeois to bohemian
Be it known

Yours Truly,

You trouble me too much.

In Other Words

One of the first English textbooks
I remember
stating
a cock means a rooster.

In those old days
only the rich owned *dickeys*—
the *trunk* that moves in a body with wheels
deriding bikers and hawkers alike.

Four letter words existed
only in the realm of a dictionary—
unspeakable meant anything but ordinary.

Fucking is what people in the ghettos did.
Dirty word.
Making love meant babies.
A woman meant not much
on her own,
or when left alone.

ELIZABETH WALLACE

Elizabeth Wallace is a Canadian psychiatrist who has practiced in Toronto and Hong Kong. She was educated at the University of Calgary and the University of Toronto. She has received national awards for her published work in the areas of psychotherapy and psychoanalysis, and has a special interest in psychoanalysis and film.

Her long latent interest in creative writing blossomed after moving to Houston with her family in 1998. She discovered poetry through workshops at Inprint taught by Derick Burleson, Michael Lieberman, and Alan Ainsworth. She also completed a poetry mentorship with Martha Rhodes through Gemini Ink in San Antonio. She was named a Juried Poet at the Houston Poetry Fest 2002, and her work has appeared in *Houston Poetry Review*. Her favorite poets include Elizabeth Bishop, Emily Dickinson, Jane Kenyon, and Mary Oliver, while her major poetic inspiration and support has come from fellow poets at Inprint.

"My passion for poetry is interwoven with my other passions – my family and my work. I am fascinated to hear people speaking poetry as they describe themselves, their dreams, and their inner lives, and to discover the unconscious at work in poems I read and write. My relationships, past and present, are the sources of my poetry, and I find poetry a powerful means to fathom more about myself and others."

BIT PARTS

Sometimes a supporting actor
appears—

say, a great-uncle who

smokes Players cigarettes,
brings you lariats
to practice rope tricks,
a baton to flip,
climbs telephone poles
with special spiked soles,
writes curling pages of poems—

to play the parts that the leads
in your life never
could.

REMEDIES

As water hyacinths surround
our boat in Jean Lafitte Park
the swamp man explains

how these waxy Japanese plants
were brought in to cleanse
murky waterways

how instead they grew
into dense unexpected
flotillas of weed

how nutria from Argentina
were imported to eat
up the surfacing mess

how they then ate
everything else, including
the sugar cane

how there is now a varmint bounty
though the swamp man tosses them
marshmallows, just the same

I take your hand and recall
how once I believed
that love could eradicate need.

HUMMING BIRDS

My mother planted blue
delphinium for bait
so we could see them right
outside the window, through
the sheer ruffle-hemmed
net curtain, through the fine
grid of screen speckled
pane, the leafy wave
of peony, lily, and rose.

The hummers rose deep-
throated—she told me
some were just the size
of thimbles—beckoning
first with whir of soft,
millisecond wings
that brought her running

just to see a stir of azure
love tunnels, blur
of iridescent green,
a slash of throat red
as needle beaks sucked
sweet honey-blood my mother
grew for them, ounces
of exotic flesh aquiver
for an instant beyond
her gray kitchen.

SHELLING

We shelled peas to her stories,
pots between knees,
kids unstringing crisp pods
of fleshy beads dropped raw
to metal bowls, sometimes a
mouth.

Grandmother shelled words,
dropped seeds into ears,
fresh plots that filled
to staccato of sweet pearls
falling,

ricocheting, sometimes spilling when,
breathless, we gasped as one
at malevolent fairies, magic mice
or birds of prophecy, fingers flipping
juice to her incantations, our bodies
just shells
shelling, as we flew
away,

from bruised linoleum,
fly specks, peeling screen door,
old skins thrown to floored paper
to fill waiting hogs—
pots, children, pigs all filling—
her story always ending
precisely
as the last shell
opened.

PARTY LINE

Each house had its ring—
ours was two longs, and a
short. (I still answer it
in dreams.)

Line busy? my dad would boom
in his big farmer voice into
the black wall box,
alerting the neighbors,
thirteen on this string.

But even my father learned
to wait, to hesitate
a few breaths before
talk, letting midair
words drop
like rain into eaves,

catching hints
of arguments, price
of cream, who went to town
with whom, whose
hand was lopped off
by a machine

as sentences swept
downstream swelling electric
flooding modest
homes and wetting
curiosity before the soaps
were ever invented.

DOUBLE DUTCH

I was the champion, second grade
        diva of skipping on concrete
squares, two ropes, first one,
        then the other in rapid
succession, feet together,
        always even, never odd
numbers, jumping from one
        friend to another
triangle, unstable threes,
        stick to the pairs
under double ellipses of dare.

I learned to jump from one
        red electric arc to another
double dilemma— win
        or lose, shine or
disappear over the slap
        of a rope, sweaty girls
counting by two's too
        dangerous
to fall or fly, pounding
        out a space for my
body that hung
        in the balance.

SEPARATING

I watched my father
sit on the three-legged stool,
his head pressed into rounded underbelly,
sending streams of warm milk pinging
into aluminum buckets, brimming,
squirted steaming onto pink cat tongues,
sometimes he even let me give the rubbery teats a try.

I watched my father
carry sloshing silvery pails
with swooshing rubber boot steps
across a muddy yard, overalls fraying,
clinking onto the cement steps with a flourish
as the screen door creaked open for flies,
and my grandfather polished up the separator.

I watched my father
heft and pour fragrant speckled white
into the huge bowl atop the shiny machine,
plug it in and what a clanging racket
as thick cream spurted from one spout
and bluish skim from the other,
cooling side by side on the milk house floor.

I watched my father
pull apart the contraption,
pour boiling kettle water on every piece,
(they still smelled like grass to me)
and lay them out to dry on clean white
tea towels, like sterile surgical instruments,
for all the milk I would never drink.

LAND SIGNS

My father's plow churned up
not just black dirt and accursed stones—
the kind that bent blades—
but arrowheads, hammerheads,
even a shriveled pemmican.

I loved those field prizes he spied
glinting and toted home to me— booty bagged
and displayed, reminders of pierced bodies
felled at the point of a hunter.
I reveled in warm, bloody hides,
past erupting through the skin
of the land in shards, like memory rent
by a flinty word or gutting gaze.

I pressed my flesh against
each chipped edge, felt the trace
of leathered hands stashing meat,
chiseling missiles that seeded
soil not fully my father's, nor my own.

So often I tilled his words
for clues to his mind— so few
to find. Looked for glint of eye,
searched his furrowed skin,
weathered and impenetrable, for telling signs.

But I felt the heaviness
of scarred rock, petrified
clots of blueberries saved
for winters long before
in wordless bits and pieces.

N̲AUTILUS

*As it grows, its shell adds new chambers;
it always lives in the largest, newest one.*

It is time, yet she shrinks back
to the familiar chamber, caressing
scars of walls pressed on her
body, once made to measure, now
bearing imprints, confinements.
She once poured her self into this.

Too late to retract the contract she has
made with her latest creation.
(Must she slither through another
one-way valve of time?)

A new room. No, room
reminds her too much of womb,
or tomb, the windowless
price she has paid
to be held. She prefers
une chambre—
its curtained consonants,
carpets of soft vowels.

So she shoehorns past the loving
impedimentia, the seductive mold.
Crosses the threshold—
will she dissolve in space?

She cannot gauge her edges
in this place, ungrazed by walls.
And for a time curls
into the old comma-
shape, filled with pain of expanse.
A spiral progress.

Finally gazing at her larger
luminous case—the kind
she always makes,
parent-of-pearl that she is,

she recalls—
oh, at first it is always
like this. As her cramped
flesh spreads, as her soles
stretch over fresh ground,

as the limits loom
far beyond she throws
back her head and laughs,
listening to the sound
of echoes heard
again, and never
the same.

THE UNMADE

To me, the ultimate disorder.
I require smooth quilt and pillows
cased in daylight.

Otherwise, the rumpled sheets
appear again in crease of sleeves
or crumpled newspaper.

Driving, I turn and shift
restless as the dented bed
spreads before me in heaves
of pavement. I hear faults speak
whirring asphalt secrets.

I read the lines of day,
glimpse wrinkles between
reminding me that night is not over,
dreams not tucked to mitred corners.

Loose blankets, loose thoughts
flap as I blow through streets,
flow across a cloud-scudded sky–

another rough terrain
of linen–

Unmade decisions,
cumulus doubt.

SHAPE CAKE

       I can shape
a cake for him
       I can bake
layers, cut corners, ice over
bumps and attach
finger biscuit boards with sweet pitch
erect pretzel masts

       I can mask
crumbs with glue
frost mistakes

       Raise a Jolly Roger

I can hang
it all together
in a masterful cut and paste
       Yes, I can make
a chocolate boat floating on blue coconut waves.

       I can shape
a cake but I cannot erase
piracy, ease pitched competition
(Child three, he must steal
to get what he needs)

       I can map
his cake but not how
he tastes it, eats it
whether he discovers
what is buried chest deep.